basic Vocal Workout

Printed and bound in the United Kingdom by Antony Rowe Limited, Chippenham, Wiltshire

Published by SMT, an imprint of Sanctuary Publishing Limited, Sanctuary House, 45-53 Sinclair Road, London W14 0NS, United Kingdom

www.sanctuarypublishing.com

Cover image courtesy of Getty Images

ISBN: 1-84492-024-0

basic Vocal Workout

Roger Kain

CONTENTS

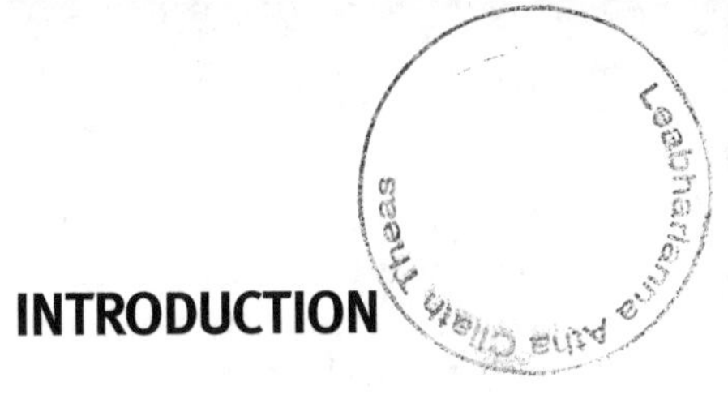

INTRODUCTION

This book is aimed at singers working on their own, but also at singing teachers, to provide a scheme of exercises designed to produce modern rock and pop sounds and ranges. At the time of writing, there is no other such scheme available. In this book I have notated the exercises in the conventional way in order to make them accessible for singing lessons and to enable teachers to expand on them.

Modern commercial singing is a highly professional and skilled occupation. It covers a wide variety of styles, including rock, metal, grunge, pop, etc, each with an enormous range of sounds and pitches. Between these classifications are the subdivisions: hard rock, soft rock, melodic rock, heavy metal, death metal, grunge metal – does anyone remember thrash? Indie? Garage? The name of each genre varies with changing times and fashions, so for the purposes of this book I shall use the generic terms, *rock* and *pop* to mean all of these styles, as these names do not seem to change.

The one obvious thing these different styles have in common is that they are totally different from opera or any other 'classical' style of singing. The sound is different, the technique is different, the range is different, the pronunciation is different. Indeed, the thinking is different, so the training has to be different. Opera isn't a good preparation for rock singing – the operatic range isn't big enough. Neither can rock singers be divided into the classical divisions of soprano, mezzo-soprano, contralto, tenor, baritone and bass – each female singer has to cover the entire female range and each male singer has to cover the entire male range.

One of the problems of teaching rock singers is that rock and pop have given rise to a new breed of feeble singing teachers who do not know enough. Many of them will tell you that you will never get up to a G or an A 'because you're a baritone or a mezzo. Only tenors or sopranos can go that high.' As if being a tenor or a soprano were somehow especially virtuous! As a matter of fact, the tenor and baritone ranges are the same, and most mezzos can sing soprano perfectly well. Similarly, any decent baritone should be able to hit a top C, which annoys the tenors who can't! I was trained as a baritone, I am well over 50, and I can still sing a perfectly good top C, while I can also sing a good bottom C, three octaves below. The difference is in the *sound*, not in the range. Many of my students can encompass an even bigger range than I can, but they were stretched earlier than I was. This process usually takes about four years, although some of my luckier students have managed it more quickly.

The worrying thing is that most singing teachers have learned nothing from the heavy-metal boom of the '70s, '80s and '90s. That phenomenal development in singing was led by singers, not teachers. They achieved their spectacular results largely by disobeying their teachers, who no doubt continued to wag their fingers, uttering dire warnings of the ruin that their charges were inflicting on their voices. The vast ranges of singers like Skye, Skin, Sebastian Bach, Michael Bolton, David Coverdale, Stephen Tyler, Jeff Tate *et al* (the list is enormous!) has meant nothing to most teachers. Throughout the whole of the last 20 years, teachers have been saying things like 'His voice is going' about each of the great heavy-metal singers – and they're still saying it. Yet these singers are still going strong, a fact which many teachers fail to notice.

Then there's the other great finger-wagging phrase, usually uttered in deep, slow lugubrious tones: '(S)he's had a few problems with his/her voice.' So what? Every singer in the world has had trouble with 'the voice' at one time or another. It's called being human.

One of the purposes of this book is to dispel some of the myths and fears of rock singing. If you hear a rock singer doing something wonderful, the chances are that you too are capable of it. Great rock singers have nothing that you don't have, physically. Perhaps they have more will power, a better 'ear', or more of the actors' instinct than you. That is dependent on your mind. A good teacher should be able to help you sort out the mental approach.

You go to a teacher mainly for three reasons:

- To find out what is available to you. A lot of songs you'll want to sing are very difficult, particularly those with very high notes, and you might start to wonder if it will ever be possible for you to sing them. Unfortunately, there are always a lot of teachers ready to tell you, 'It's out of your range.' They will usually follow this up with two insidious statements: 'If you try to force the voice up, you'll do permanent damage' and 'Anyone who tells you that you can get up to these notes is a liar.' This is nothing less than moral blackmail designed to hide the teacher's lack of knowledge. If a teacher says, 'You can't go that high because you're [or you're not] this, that or the other, it probably means, 'I don't know how to teach you to sing up there.' There are perfectly safe ways of opening up recalcitrant high notes, and this book contains exercises for several different approaches (I'm not bigoted). Even most true basses – the rarest voice of all – can eventually reach a top C and high sopranos can build up a chest voice capable of sustaining a gutsy bottom E (below middle C).

- To tap into the accumulated knowledge of centuries. This is often the giveaway that great singers have had singing lessons: they know too much to have been self-taught. There are techniques available for solving every single problem in singing, including the development of a good chest voice for singers who think they can't get deep notes and the opening up of a glorious head voice for singers who keep hitting that 'ceiling'. These are common problems. What makes them serious is that they tend to induce a mental block. If you can't hit the notes your heroes are singing, it's probably because you haven't found the right technique – and maybe your singing teacher hasn't, either!

- To deal with the psychological problems of singing. Or, to put it in modern terms, to sort out the mind-set, the mental blocks, the fear of auditions, the fear of meeting the band for the first time, the fear of high notes, the fear of looking a prat, the fear of letting go so that you always hold back on notes that you should really just go for. You want that wonderful high note, and you know you can do it, but every time you come to it, you hold back on it – you clench your throat immediately before you try to sing it, strangling it. But the damage is done before you utter a sound.

  To make matters worse, somebody will tell you that it's out of your range. The real problem here is that high notes are terrifying, but you *know* that fear is something to be dealt with; you *know* that you shouldn't give in to it.

The art of singing involves the emotions more than any other form of music-making. You are your own instrument. You must make all your notes. You are totally responsible for the quality of all of the sounds that you produce, in a way that instrumentalists are not, and that is a terrifying responsibility. It makes you vulnerable. As you approach difficult notes, they can almost seem to be lying in wait for you, like time bombs ticking away. All sorts of questions run through your mind:

- Am I going to hit that note?
- Is it going to go wrong?
- Can the neighbours hear me?
- Is it going to hurt my throat?
- Could I sing it quietly, so that nobody will hear me missing it?

You feel you can be blamed for every sound that isn't perfect. That's pressure! It's not like pressing a switch or depressing a key on a keyboard. You can press down the highest key on a keyboard and the highest note will come out, easily, perfectly. If it doesn't, you can blame the sound engineer. It's no hardship for the keyboard player. But for you to sing your highest possible note is traumatic. It's frightening. It can also be incredibly exciting.

You'll have problems with sore throats, certainly at the beginning – the early-day sore throat – and also with colds in the early stages. All singers do. I won't be dealing with those ailments here.

The real message of this introduction is this: Don't concern yourself with what you *can* do; concentrate on what you *want* to do.

Written Music

To be able to sing at sight (that means first sight!) is the most lucrative skill in music. A studio will pay a huge recording fee for a singer who can pick up a sheet of new music (which might be thick with harmonies) and sing it accurately, in the right sounds, straight away – that's professionalism – so it's worthwhile building up your skills.

Reading music frightens many singers, but it's really not very difficult. All you need to know is your alphabet from A to G and how to count up to 13. Even if you can't be precise about it at first, you can see when the dots (noteheads) go up and down, so your voice should go up or down correspondingly, and you can estimate at a glance from the spacing how long to hold each note. I'm not exaggerating – that really covers all that music involves. If in doubt, you can always make an intelligent guess! Written music is entirely logical, unlike learning languages, all of which are illogical (some more so than others) and require you to learn far more information than reading music does. The best way to learn to read music is to learn to play keyboards. This will very quickly give you an understanding of the complete structure of music.

Now, although it's not strictly necessary for a singer to be able to read music or to play keyboards, most successful singers can do both. A lot of them paid for their first bands and demos out of the proceeds of session singing and playing. In general, the more you know, the better equipped you are to succeed and to remain successful.

This is where I appear to contradict myself. Earlier, I said that written music is entirely logical, and this is true, but the *conventions* of written music for voices are a bit confused. Usually, the female voice is written in the treble clef at the actual pitch (ie the pitch that is sung), but not always. Sometimes, for convenience, it's written an octave higher or lower. Don't worry about that.

In contrast, conventions of notation for the male voice are in a right old historical muddle. Sometimes it's written in the bass clef and should be sung at the written pitch, while at other times it's written in the treble clef, usually (but not always) to be sung an octave lower than written. None of these strange conventions makes music-reading any more difficult. You get used to them.

basic Vocal Workout

In order to avoid confusion, all of the exercises in this book are written at their actual pitches, whether in the bass or treble clef, except where the guidance notes specifically state otherwise.

1 THE RANGE

The first thing to notice about the vocal range is that it is very wide. The notation on the next couple of pages isn't a misprint; many modern rock singers really can cover that range. This wouldn't be possible for anyone trained only in the classical tradition, and it was certainly not thought possible before about 1970. Singing teachers at that time were extremely wary of men who wanted to extend their range upwards and women who wanted to extend their chest voices downward, and indeed many still are – they usually described it as 'forcing the voice'. However, as you go through the exercises contained in this book, you'll find that there's no need to force the voice. You will find it extremely hard work, but *hard work* is not the same as *forcing*.

It was the emergence of heavy metal that brought about the extension of the vocal range. The sound of the bands became so hard and piercing that singers made a terrible discovery: microphones do not turn a woolly sound into a well-focused sound; they only transmit what the singer puts into them. Singers were being

The Range Of The Rock Voice

Showing what becomes possible when you can mix the voices. These are all notated at *actual pitch*.

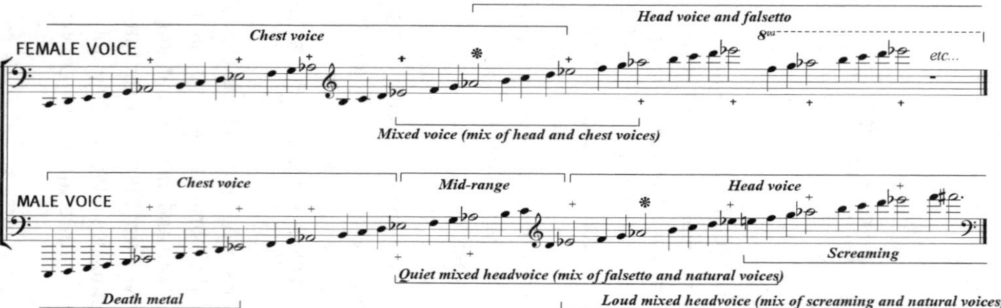

❋ **A♭**, the note on which all voices change dramatically. In a woman's voice it is the dividing line between the head and chest voices. It is called the *passaggio*. By extending the chest voice upwards and the head voice downwards, it is possible to achieve a wide overlap and choose the note on which to change voices and, eventually, to develop a smooth mixed voice. Some men have difficulty in singing above this note, but every man can, including a true bass, the rarest male voice of all.

\+ The changes in the voice are invariably on **A♭** and **E♭**. These are usually small changes, but they can become serious divisions if the technique is not right for that pitch.

By Contrast, The Well-Developed Classical Ranges

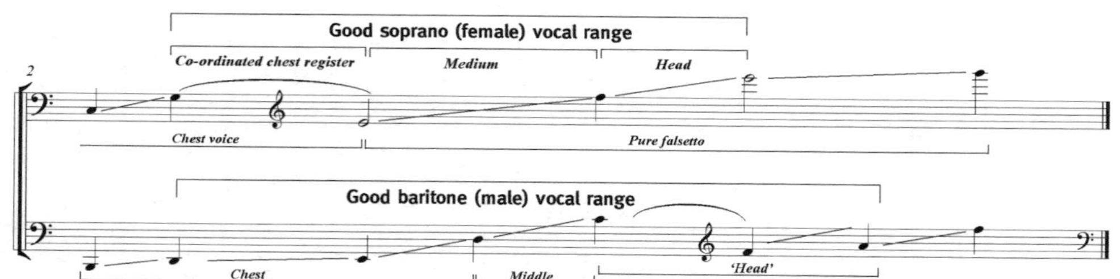

Given in *Bel Canto: Principles And Practices* by Cornelius L Reid (New York, 1950, pp 89-91). This has been largely ignored by teachers who thought it was hopelessly ambitious, that you couldn't sing both high and low, but Professor Reid was right. If anything, he *underestimated* what was possible. I exercise nearly all male singers to the extremities of this range from the first lesson. They are usually surprised that they can do it, and without ill effects.

Examples Of Poor Ranges

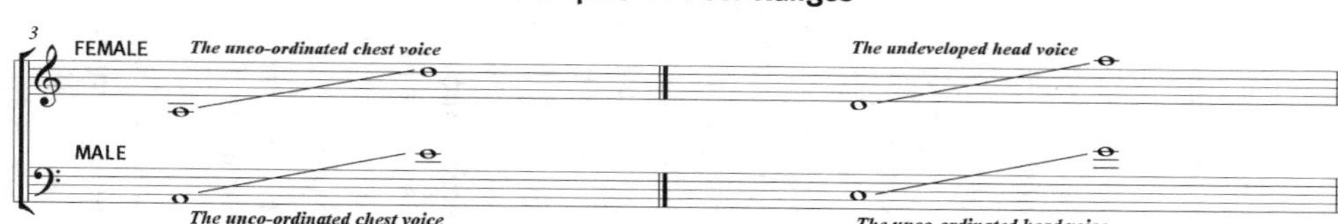

drowned out. They had to find a way of cutting through the backing or riding over it. Men mostly rode over it by going higher and louder, and singing above A♭ (the start of the second register of the natural head voice), where most men can produce a voice that is indestructible. It's very difficult for most men to get into that register, but all men can, even true basses.

Women's voices don't work in quite the same way. The strategy employed by most women was to open up the deep resonance of the chest voice, producing a massive sound, and then to extend it upwards as far as possible. For most women, that means up to E♭ in the top space of the treble clef. A lot of women also wanted the highest possible notes of the head voice, where outrageousness is very exciting. In the process, both men and women discovered that their voices doubled in power right down through the range to the very lowest notes, which became known as *death-metal notes*. With this, another interesting fact emerged: singers who can go highest are often the same singers who can go lowest. Don't believe anyone who says that you can't sing both high and low – you can. It might take a few years, but the techniques for it are all presented in this book.

Some singing teachers and voice experts predicted that these heavy-metal singers would ruin their voices in five minutes, when in fact the reverse happened: the more they extended their ranges, the better their voices became. The empirical evidence is now overwhelming: singers who extend their ranges improve as they get older, while singers who don't...don't. They either hang on or they deteriorate. Most of the great heavy-metal singers of the '70s are still big names, and their voices are still improving. The interesting fact that emerges is this: the massive improvements in singing were made by performers who disobeyed their teachers.

The second thing to notice is that the voice changes on A♭ and E♭. It's the same for everybody, and it never varies. This is a useful fact to know when you're trying to work out why your voice seems to be refusing to do what (or sound the way) you want it to.

2 OPENING UP THE VOICE

Basic Exercises For Power And Range

Why Do Exercises At All? Why Not Just Sing Songs?

Exercises are targeted at problem solving in a way that songs are not. A lot of songs are very good exercises in their own right, but that isn't their main purpose. Exercises should do two things. Firstly, they should stretch you, which will help you to get at the notes and sounds that excite you. Secondly, they should build up good habits so that your technique becomes automatic. In other words, exercises help you to cope with your voice under any circumstance. Whatever your problem, there's an exercise to solve it.

Getting Started

The first and, indeed, one of the most difficult things to do is to try to get some high notes. You'll find that, after singing high notes, your whole voice will be much brighter than it was before, all the way down (unless you try to do it from the throat – that would be disastrous). High notes stretch the soft palate, and they are also exhilarating. You also need some notes in reserve, and so, however high you go in your songs, to make them secure you need to try to go even higher in exercises. Don't be put off by people who say, 'Stick to your natural range,' whatever that may be! If you give up on high notes just because they're more difficult than low notes, you'll never achieve anything. As long as you follow the step-by-step guidance notes listed here, you'll be all right.

You don't have to get everything right straight away. You should be able to get up to A♭ (Exercise 1, bar 6), but don't worry if you can't. Do as much as you can. Tomorrow's another day.

Exercise 1: Making A Start On The High Notes

This is the perfect exercise with which to start your warm-up.

GUIDANCE NOTES

This exercise is *loud*. if you try to do it quietly, you won't get up to the top notes – at least, not in the right voice. Top notes are louder than bottom notes. This is particularly important for men – women can sometimes get away with quiet top notes as long as they can get hold of them. But the general rule is to go a little bit louder (sometimes a *lot* louder) when you go up; you can usually let the notes look after themselves when you come down.

Keep the tip of the tongue against the bottom teeth. This is very important indeed, as it will stop you putting pressure on the throat and will focus your voice, making singing a lot easier. When the tongue goes back or is left flapping in mid-air, it's usually because you're clenching the base of the tongue. The antidote is to place the tip against something at the front of the mouth, preferably the bottom teeth or the bottom gum.

Take in as big a breath as you can manage with the diaphragm (in practice, that really means your stomach) before you sing. As you hit the highest note in each phrase (accented ^), pull the diaphragm in hard and take the strain with the stomach. (See Exercise 2, 'Learning To Control The Breath'.)

There must be no pressure on the neck, no veins or arteries standing out like drainpipes. They will stop you getting up to your highest notes, I guarantee it. High notes take a lot of effort, a lot of struggle. You must take the strain with the diaphragm. If your neck hurts but your diaphragm doesn't, you're not doing enough with the diaphragm.

If this doesn't work, there's another technique: constipate the note. This is an instruction my first singing teacher gave me. It has rescued my students (and me) from a lot of difficulties over the years. As you go for the top note, pull in the diaphragm – and try to push it out through your bottom. To put it another way, for top notes, go for a fart! It's better than straining the neck.

Women shouldn't try to sing it all in the big, gutsy chest voice; let it go into the head voice, or falsetto voice. You need these notes. Don't worry about it sounding girly or classical or squeaky or silly – that doesn't matter. You must exercise the head voice if you want the chest voice to work really well for you.

Men, however, should keep it all in the natural voice. Don't let it go into falsetto at all. That means *keep it loud*. There's no way of getting a Top B or a Top C quietly, at least not until you're very experienced.

basic Vocal Workout

Steady 4, strong, driving rhythm.

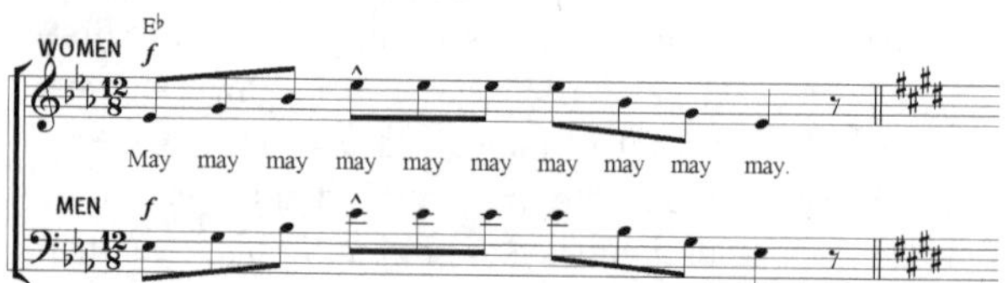

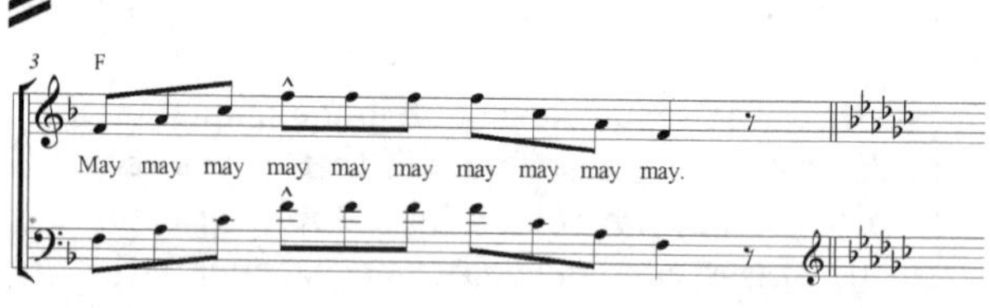

5
G
May may may may may may may may may may.
6
A♭
May may may may may may may may may may.
Don't worry if you can't go as high as this; it's very difficult for some singers. Do as much as you can today. There's another day tomorrow.
7
Women, let it go into head voice (falsetto)
A
May may may may may may may may may may.
Men, do NOT let it go into falsetto
8
B♭
May may may may may may may may may may.
9
B
May may may may may may may may may may.

10 C
May may may may may may may may may may.
11 D♭
May may may may may may may may may may.
It's unlikely that many men will be able to sing as high as this. If you can, keep going.
Ladies continue:
12 D
May may may may may may may may may may.
13 E♭
May may may may may may may may may may.
14 E
May may may may may may may may may may.
15 F
May may may may may may may may may may.

Exercise 2: Learning To Control The Breath

You don't need to be a genius to realise that this subject is very important to any singer. You don't want to be approaching your big note only to find that you've run out of breath at the crucial moment. But what you might not realise is that you need extra breath in reserve to *support* your top notes. If your high notes are going flat, it might mean that you need a bigger breath than you thought you did.

Most people misunderstand the phrases 'breathe in' and 'breathe out'; they get them the wrong way around. When you breathe in deeply, the base of your lungs gets bigger – like a balloon. When you breathe out, it gets smaller – flat, like an empty balloon.

The basic technique is this: you breathe with the diaphragm. Think of it as breathing with your stomach. You do *not* breathe with your neck – there should be no movement there at all. This enables you to store air in the base of the lungs. When you use it to support high notes or power singing, this air becomes compressed and very strong, like the air in the inner tube of a car tyre – the whole car is supported on compressed air, and this is the type of power-house you need to build in order to support your voice. What you'll now have worked out (and I'm sure you're there before me) is that not only does the diaphragm control the breathing, but also that the diaphragm has no power to do *anything* unless you take in a big enough breath in the first place. What happy logic!

GUIDANCE NOTES

Sit in an upright chair (office or dining type) and lean back without lifting its front legs off the floor. Place one hand *lightly* around the front of your neck and the other hand on your stomach – that is, the base of your lungs, your diaphragm. This is where you're going to do most of the work.

Now breathe out. That means, expel all the air by pulling the diaphragm in as far as you can. Use your hand to help it. Now breathe in, puffing up the lower part of your stomach like a balloon, so that it pushes your hand out.

All this must be done *without moving your neck at all*. You should be able to detect unwanted movement with the hand placed lightly on your neck. Do this for a few minutes each day. Get used to breathing as deeply as possible, moving the stomach as much as possible with each breath (it should move about five inches) with no movement in the neck or throat at all.

You may well experience dizziness. This is quite normal, it probably means that you're breathing more deeply than you've ever done before. This is a good sign. Pause until it passes. You will adjust very quickly. What makes you dizzy today won't do so in a few weeks' time.

Exercise 3: An Easy Way To Start Opening Up The Low Notes

The object of this exercise is to get the lowest possible notes by relaxing. Low notes are easy – as long as you don't force them and you're patient. Nevertheless, they might take a while. Every singer has both a head voice and a chest voice; this means that everybody can eventually sing both high notes and low notes. You need to exercise both of them because they both have a lot to contribute to the sound of the whole voice. You need the low notes, even if you never intend to sing any low numbers, as they improve the tone of the whole voice and stop your high notes from sounding shrill or strident.

Specifically, women need the low notes so that they can extend the chest voice upwards and build up the power in the middle of the voice. This, of course, is essential if you want to compete with the big stars.

Men need the low notes to give the middle register a

bit of 'bite'. Most men have a problem in the middle of the voice, which is often weak. If you force these notes, you'll lose all of your high notes. The weakness is due to half of the voice being under-developed, usually the chest voice. What you need to do is work patiently on extending your lowest notes. But – and I cannot repeat it often enough – don't force them; open up your throat and let them start developing in the following way:

GUIDANCE NOTES

Keep the notes very short and make sure all the Hs are crisp, short and clear, or you'll find your throat taking an active part in the proceedings, and you don't want that. You should bypass the throat by keeping it wide open and focusing the sound in the nose. Let the sound sail through your mouth without touching the sides, so to speak.

The pronunciation should be very open, ie 'Ha!' as in *hat*, not 'Haw' as in *law* – these sounds are too closed and operatic. They'll probably knock you out of tune before you're halfway down.

Push the jaw right down, keeping the mouth open wide, like a yawn. The tip of the tongue should be against the bottom teeth – this is always a good way of keeping the voice off the throat and of focusing it in the nose.

Start loudly. Keep your head down. Ease off the volume when you get really low, or when the tuning becomes difficult.

Now you might encounter a problem in switching from very low notes to very high notes. The secret is this: If you were using the throat to produce the sounds in Exercise 3, you might experience difficulty in getting up to the high notes in Exercise 4, but if you follow the Guidance Notes, keeping the pressure off the throat, you should have no difficulty at all in switching directly to the high notes.

basic Vocal Workout

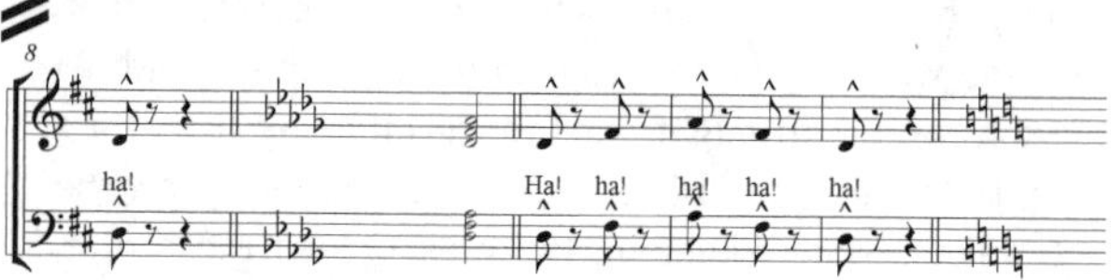

GUIDANCE NOTES (CONTINUED)

At this pitch, you might be finding it difficult to relax. Perhaps your jaw is becoming stiff, or the notes are less easy to control. If so, you can now change the technique. Start easing your head right back, and feel your whole throat opening up. Push your jaw right down with the tip of your tongue, and feel the notes focusing, gently and effortlessly, in the bridge of your nose.

Make sure you're not pulling your head back into your neck – that will cause a lot of tightness. The lower you sing, the more open and relaxed you should feel.

Ease your head back (see Guidance Notes above). Keep the notes short and crisp.

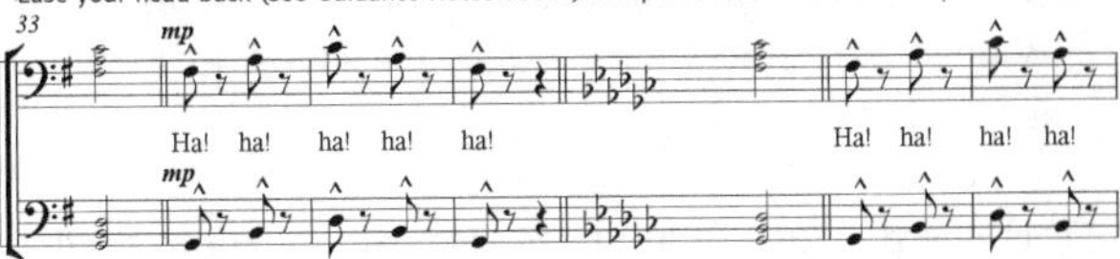

Continue very gently down to here, if you can. Nearly all singers can get down to these pitches, if they take the head back far enough, relax enough and feel the entire throat open enough.

Don't force these notes.

To be sung an octave lower than written (note the figure eight below the clef).

Exercise 4: A Second Go At The High Notes – Improving The Tone

GUIDANCE NOTES

Because this consists mostly of downward scales, with an introductory note leading up to the top note, you need to concentrate on only the first two notes. Let the downward notes look after themselves; just keep them in tune.

This is a particularly loud exercise; do not try to do it quietly. Take in a big breath with the diaphragm (that means puff out the stomach) and pull it in for the highest note in each phrase (the note with the ^ symbol over it).

Pronunciation

- **Too-wee** – These two sounds (which are very easy) both have closed vowels, and this seems to cause people a lot of psychological problems. They don't trust them, so they tend to sing 'toe-way'. Stick your lips out for 'too' – this forms a tunnel going both forward and backward down the throat, and is very good for resonance. For 'wee', pull the corners of your lips back into a forced smile. This serves to focus the voice onto the hard palate, making the sound very bright, particularly on the high notes.

- **No Hs** – The temptation to use Hs to separate the notes in the downward scales seems irresistible to a lot of my students, probably because they can't quite shake the habit of doing things, or defining things, with the throat. In this exercise, Hs very quickly turn themselves into glottal stops, and singers find themselves coughing their way down the scales.

- **Don't avoid the W** – People tend to think this is intrusive. In fact, it is essential for smoothness.

- Men should not go into falsetto at all in this exercise.

basic Vocal Workout

Pull in the diaphragm on notes accented ^

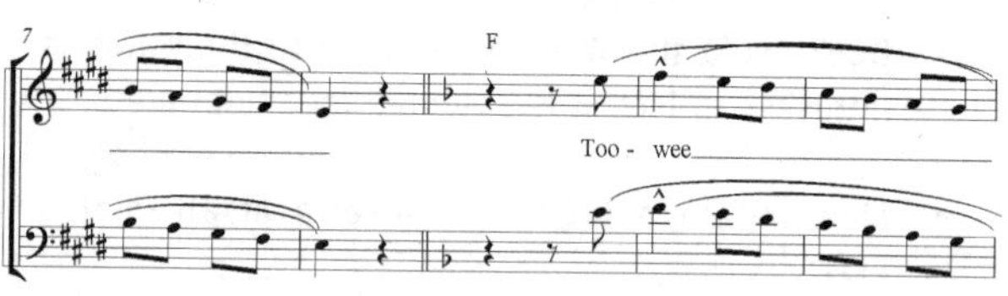

Opening Up The Voice

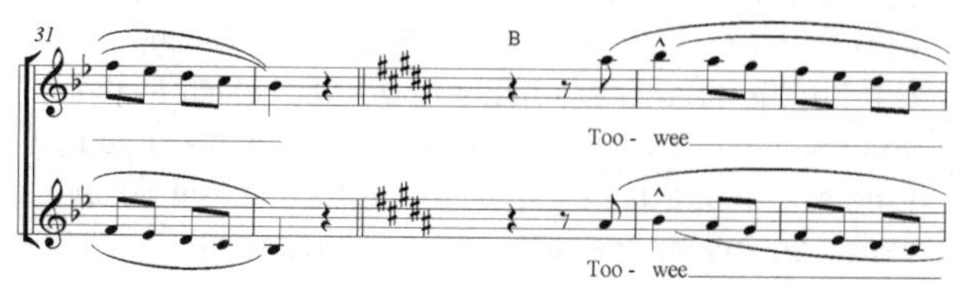

Exercise 5: Smoothing Over The Joins In The Female Voice

This isn't a big, belting exercise, unlike most of my exercises; this is for fine-tuning and smoothing over the *passaggio*.

GUIDANCE NOTES

This exercise is in two parts: (a) the staccato version and (b) the legato version. Although it appears to be lightweight and trivial, this is the most important exercise of all. It solves most of the problems of tuning and smoothes over all the 'breaks'. This exercise is, in fact, at least 300 years old. It is very simple and effective.

Watch the tuning. Be precise about every note, especially the second note of each scale, which, you will find, is particularly liable to go flat, which in this context means that the pitch is slightly too low. If your tuning is suspect, help the first note (marked ^) by gently squeezing the diaphragm to support it.

Keep it all quiet, but don't let it become inaudible. Keep the notes well-focused right to the end.

In the staccato version, keep it all very crisp. Let the voice change where it wants to; don't try to do it all in one voice or the other.

In the legato version, keep it very smooth indeed, with no jolts. Smoothness is everything.

If you find yourself running out of breath, take a bigger breath with the diaphragm and squeeze *all the air out* on the last two or three notes of each phrase. That will force you to take a big breath for the next phrase.

You need both halves of the voice to work, and you need to be able to join them up. The higher you can start this exercise, the better. Surprisingly, most of the problems in the middle of the voice can be solved by working downward from your highest possible notes.

(a) Staccato Version

(b) Legato Version

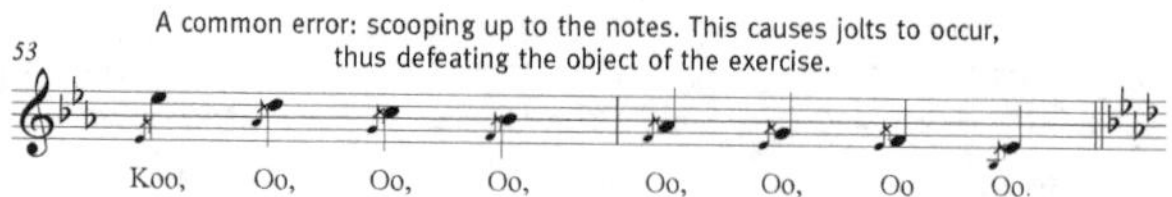

At the second or third lesson, if the first scale (E♭) has been succesful, try starting from here:

And, at a later lesson, from here...

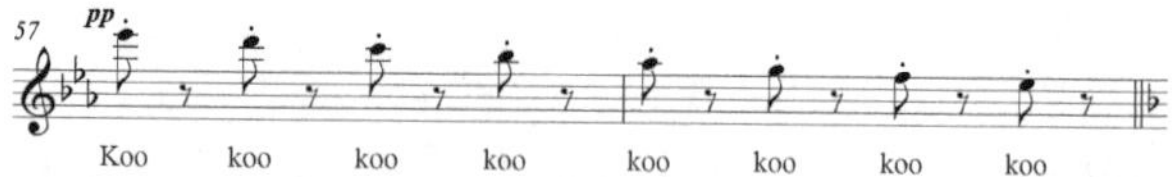

...and eventually from here.

It is important to exercise these high notes so that the soft palate is stretched. This gives you control over the tone throughout the voice and also smoothes over the *passaggios*, or 'breaks'.

Always finish the entire sequence here:

Exercise 6: Joining Up The Male Voices

Although at first glance you might think this exercise is very similar to the girls' version (Exercise 5), it varies in two ways: it is loud, and the change from falsetto into the natural head voice is specific. You can try to smoothe over it, but it is very difficult; you'll have a much better chance of disguising the join (the *passaggio*) later, when we come to look at the *quiet mixed voice*. Nonetheless, the objects are to smoothe the voice down after the excesses of previous exercises, to begin the process of blending the different head voices and, most importantly, to start working the falsetto voice as early as possible.

GUIDANCE NOTES

The music for this exercise is printed at the actual pitch. It is not a misprint.

First, sing the staccato version. Starting with the A♭ major scale, bar (or measure) 1, sing the first five scales entirely in falsetto (the childish voice). You'll need to do this loudly or you won't get up to the first note. You'll also need a lot of help from the diaphragm, so pull the stomach in hard to get hold of the first note. If you can't reach the A♭, try it from the F major scale (bar 4) to get yourself started, then try the A♭ again.

When you get down to the E♭ scale (bar 6), let it change into the natural voice midway down the scale, somewhere around A♭ (the fifth note of the scale) or G (the sixth note). You may need to squeeze the diaphragm to make a smooth change. Everyone has a natural voice-change on that particular A♭, but it's often difficult to control, but this exercise is designed to help you to control it. (So always try to effect the change on A♭ or G. All scales contain one or the other, but sometimes the A♭ is called G♯.) Change higher if you can, lower if you can't.

Watch the tuning. Be precise about every note, especially the second note of each scale, which, you'll find, is particularly liable to go flat. Don't try to change voices on the second note of any scale; it will be almost impossible to keep it in tune.

From the A♭ scale (bar 13) onwards, try to do it all in the natural voice. If you can't, change on the third note, not the second. When you've done the staccato version of this exercise, have a go at the legato version.

The Trap

The Unwanted Extra Note

This is very common. Indeed, we've all done it. We have this psychological need to 'try out' difficult notes at easier pitches before we commit ourselves to the proper pitch. Obviously, it defeats the object of the exercise, which is to smoothe over the join between the falsetto and 'natural' voices, or to try to. To avoid such a trap, start by taking a bigger breath than you think you need and, just before you arrive at the change, squeeze the diaphragm, gently but firmly, and *concentrate*. You'll understand this exercise better when you work on the quiet mixed head voice, but you need to do this loud version first.

After you've worked on the quiet mixed head voice for a while, you'll no longer need to do the legato version (version [b]) of this exercise – the former exercise will take care of the smoothness – but you'll still need the staccato version (version [a]) to exercise your highest possible falsetto notes as, apart from the screaming exercises, this is the only exercise that enables you to get at them.

basic Vocal Workout

(a) Staccato Version

Read the Guidance Notes on pages 47–8 carefully.

Do the first five scales entirely in falsetto. If you can't manage the first scale straight away, start with the fourth scale.

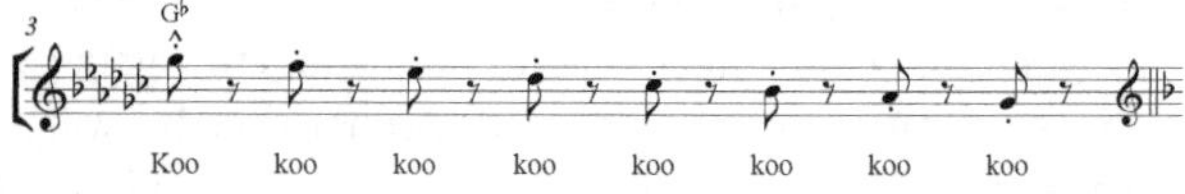

If you can't manage the higher scales, start here and then try the higher scales:

Now change from the falsetto voice into the natural voice on the note marked ❋

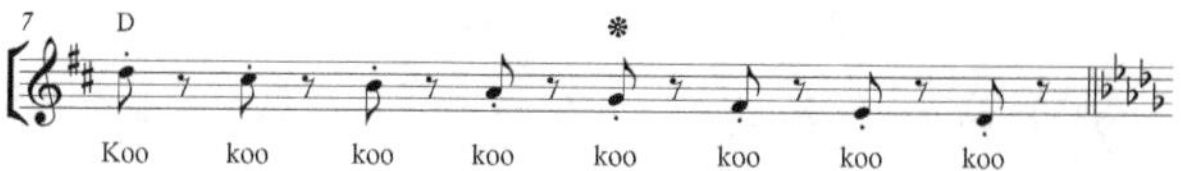

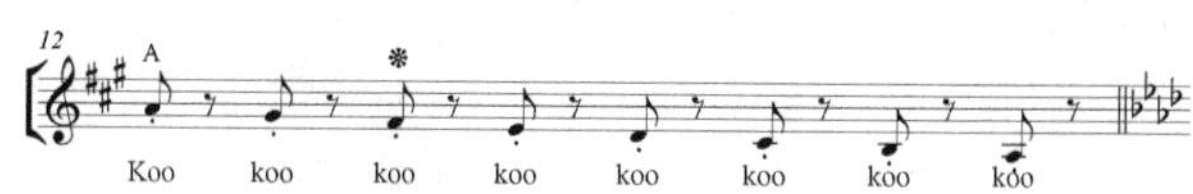

Do the remaining scales entirely in the natural voice, if you can.

(b) Legato Version

Read the Guidance Notes on pages 47–8 carefully.

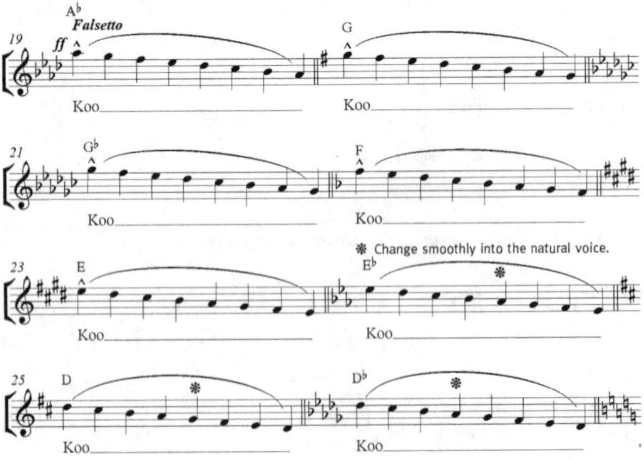

19 A♭ *Falsetto* *ff*
Koo______ G Koo______

21 G♭ Koo______ F Koo______

❋ Change smoothly into the natural voice.

23 E Koo______ E♭ ❋ Koo______

25 D ❋ Koo______ D♭ ❋ Koo______

Entirely in the natural voice from here on.

The Trap

The unwanted extra note. (Read the Guidance Notes on pages 47–8.)

Exercise 7: Pistol Shots

This is a superb way of waking up the power in the middle of the voice, but don't *start* your warm-up with this exercise; do some high-and-low exercises first.

GUIDANCE NOTES

These are short, sharp notes, as loud as you can make them. The title says it all: they should sound like pistol shots, motivated sharply from the diaphragm and focused in the nose, bypassing the throat altogether. If you use the throat, they won't sound like pistol shots at all but like growls – very unappealing. Also, they will hurt.

Take a good breath with the diaphragm, push the jaw right down, giving you plenty of space, and put the tongue firmly against the bottom teeth.

The Hs must come from the diaphragm and the voice must focus in the nose. You must do nothing with the throat but keep it open. Both Hs and vowels should be produced in one action: slam the diaphragm in sharply for the H.

Pronunciation

Ha! as in 'hat', but don't end it with a glottal stop; instead, keep the throat open. Make the sound as bright as you can. Brightness is crucial in this exercise. Make the sound brash, even brassy.

First, try it slowly without a specific pitch: '[breath] Ha! [breath] Ha! [breath] Ha!', etc.

Pistol Shots

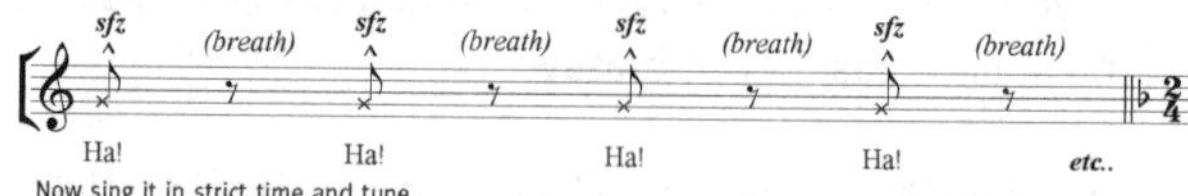

Now sing it in strict time and tune.

Ladies first.

Now the men...

The Story So Far

So, you've made a start on building up the voice. Maybe you've got everything right pretty much first time and without any real difficulty – some people do. If so, you've done very well indeed. It's much more likely, however, that you found it very difficult, that the notes you wanted remained obstinately out of reach and that the strain on your throat may make you think that all of these exercises are out of your range. You might even be wondering if you will ever be able to sing like a great rock singer. Don't be discouraged – I never promised that it would be easy. Self-doubt is almost the natural state for a singer.

Next, let's tackle the problem of excessive pressure on the throat. Ideally, there should be no veins, arteries or lumpiness showing on the outside of the neck when you sing (although at this stage, that's too much to hope for!). Instead, all of that pressure must be transferred to the power muscles, particularly the diaphragm.

Exercise 8: Co-ordinating The Power Muscles On The High Notes

GUIDANCE NOTES

This exercise is loud and mechanical – diaphragm *in* for the high notes, *out* for the low notes. In order for this to work, you *must* take a very big breath with the diaphragm: puff up your stomach like a balloon so that you have plenty to pull in for the high notes.

Keep the lips almost closed for 'mee' (try pulling the corners of the lips back into a forced smile), and the jaw should be right down for 'yaa'. The tongue should be firmly against the bottom teeth *all the time.*

Keep your head down. Sing the whole of the exercise loudly or you won't be able to control the top notes. This is true for both sexes, but particularly important for men. Women should allow the top notes to go into the head voice, but men must keep it all in the natural voice with no falsetto at all.

If you can't get down to the bottom notes, it means that you're getting stuck in the top register. You're probably locking the jaw in the halfway position, neither closed enough for 'mee' nor open enough for 'yaa'. The solution is to push the jaw right down on 'yaa' – that will usually release the lock.

Make a meal of the Y in 'yaa'. Overdo it. Wallow in it. Y is a godsend to singers; it focuses the voice wonderfully by exercising the tongue and jaw in the perfect way. When you reach the highest phrase, come back down, singing the phrases in the reverse order.

Octave Leaps

Pull the diaphragm in for the high notes (marked ^). Let it out for the low notes.

To sing higher you need to sing louder. High notes are louder than low notes, generally.

Now go back down, singing the phrases in the reverse order.

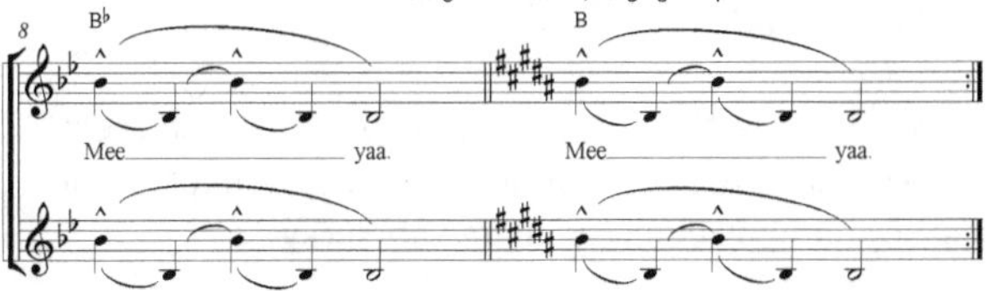

3 THE CHEST VOICE

Exercises For The Middle And Lower Notes

A good, rich, powerful and deep chest voice is very saleable – probably because it is comparatively rare among male pop or rock singers and is the most distinguishing characteristic of female rock and pop singers.

This is where the main difference lies in the female voice, between opera singing and rock. For women, opera singing takes place mostly in the head voice, even in the contralto roles, and they will put a great deal of work into bringing the sound of the sweetest head notes down into the middle register. But, for a woman, rock and pop singing is mostly in the chest voice, which needs to be powerful and should be extended as high as possible for the power, and as low as possible for the tone, so that it is rich rather than strident.

Most men are better at the head voice than the chest voice. So, if you're a man and the deep sounds come easily and powerfully, you are very lucky.

However, whether you're a man or a woman, don't be fooled into thinking that you have a naturally deep voice, or that you're a contralto or a bass just because you find low notes easier than high notes – we all do. You might be mistaking the need for hard work on the high notes for impossibility. There is an easy test: If you have a naturally resonant chest voice, it will be apparent in your speaking voice – it will be the first thing that people notice about you the first time they hear you speak. It will surprise them.

We all have a chest voice, with very deep notes available to us, but it may take a lot of patient work to open it up. Even when you're able to sing all the really low notes well, with a good, hard edge, the sound might still be thin and unresonant. You can't force low notes or they go out of tune and may even hurt; they must be exercised gently and persistently over a long period – months, or even years. If they are not exercised frequently, they will dry up and become unavailable to you temporarily, although you can get them back with a few days' work.

Even if you have a wide top register with wonderful high notes, you can still develop very good deep notes without losing anything at the top end of your voice. Contrariwise, your top notes are likely to become warmer and richer the more you develop your chest voice. Don't believe people who say that you can't sing both high and low: you can as long as you don't use your throat to produce any of the sounds.

Most of my chest-voice exercises include a lot of work either for the diaphragm or for breath control. This is very useful for the teacher, as it provides a distraction from one of the chief objectives of all these exercises: building up some resonance with prolonged use. So, while the students are struggling with endless repetitions of exercises for diaphragm agility, for instance, they are unwittingly exercising the chest voice without pressure on the throat. Also, they tend to stop worrying about their ability to sing in tune (a constant problem with many students in the early stages) and the instinct for accurate tuning takes over, usually – but not always, alas.

Exercise 9: Long Notes To Build Up Deep Sounds

Resonance and vocal technique are best developed with long notes and sustained phrases, not to mention breath control.

GUIDANCE NOTES

The object is to hold the third note – 'yaa' – loudly for at least 20 seconds.

Take a big breath, puffing up the diaphragm, and begin to sing, keeping the tongue against the bottom teeth throughout. Be very grudging, at first, about using up the breath – don't use it up all at once but, when you feel it running out, squeeze the diaphragm so that you use up all of the air. This tends to induce you to take a huge breath for the next go. By the end of the note, you may need to pull in the diaphragm so far that you feel yourself bending over. Breath control doesn't improve with age, unlike most things to do with singing, so make it as good as you can right now.

Push the jaw right down with the tip of the tongue at the *beginning* of 'yaa', not as an afterthought. This is very important, as it will focus the sound on the hard palate, but if you're doing it right it will feel as if you're focusing in the nose.

The breath will last much longer if you sing it with a good hard edge on the voice – not harsh but focused. If the sound is woolly, the breath will not last. If this happens, try singing louder.

Start with the head down. As you go lower, you'll need to ease off the volume. The printed music will tell you when to do this, but you'll probably feel when to ease off.

basic Vocal Workout

Get a good, hard edge on the sound. Focus in the nose.

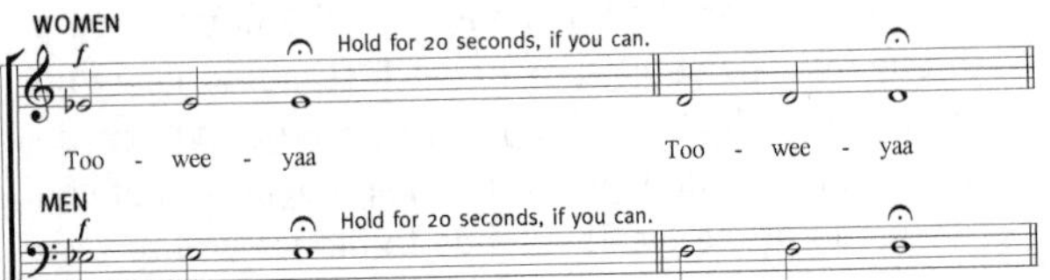

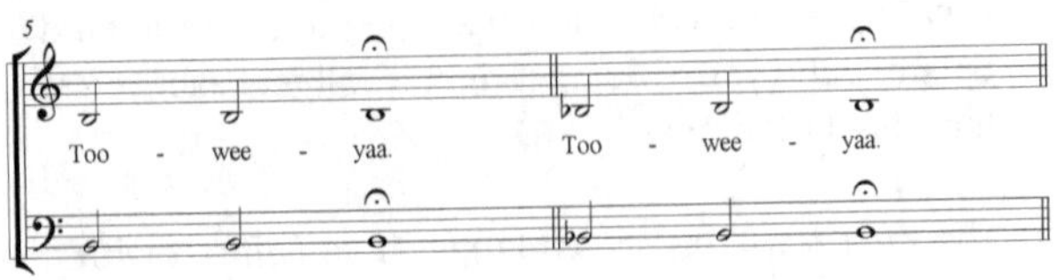

GUIDANCE NOTES (CONTINUED)

From here on, you may have difficulty in producing a convincing sound. The tuning may become awkward, you might not be able to get down to the required note, or perhaps you find yourself cramping the jaw or the root of the tongue in order to produce a hard-edged sound. If any of those happens, change the technique.

Ease your head right back. Relax. Allow your whole throat to open, as if you're a patient receiving mouth-to-mouth respiration. Sing gently. Don't try to 'make' the sound; let it grow. Still keep the tongue against the bottom teeth. Still focus in the nose.

In this, the lower half of the exercise, it can feel as if you are meditating. Sometimes it feels as if the sound is not really being made by you, but by someone else — a very pleasant feeling. If you can't get to the lowest notes (not even by doing them very quietly indeed) or can't get a good focus in the nose, don't worry; there's another day tomorrow.

Low notes should be focused, not forced.

4 THE POWER MUSCLES AND THE CHEST VOICE

All diaphragm exercises are difficult and require a lot of hard work. It's easier to learn to manipulate the diaphragm in the chest voice than in any other part of the voice, because low notes are generally easier than high notes.

These exercises are much easier to learn when you're young – in your middle teens, for instance. At that age, many students can learn these techniques in a matter of weeks. After that, it takes far more perseverance. Students in their 30s and 40s generally take a few years to learn them, but it's worth it. Once mastered, you never lose them.

There are three principal objectives here. Firstly, you need to take all the activity away from the throat, which has little stamina, and replace it with activity performed by the diaphragm, which has enormous stamina and can be trained to perform almost endlessly. Sometimes – on tour, in rehearsal, in the studio – you may have to sing for 10 or 12 hours in a day, maybe for a couple of weeks at a stretch. If you're using the throat for everything, it will be sore for a lot of that time, but if you're using the diaphragm, although you will still be tired, your singing isn't likely to let you down. Even if you go down with a cold (quite probable when you're exhausted), you may well find that your technique enables you to keep singing well – for a while.

Secondly, you need to develop the habit of working from the diaphragm so that controlling the tone and power becomes automatic.

Thirdly, you need to develop well-controlled vibrato from the diaphragm. Once you've learned how to do this, you'll never lose it, and you'll rarely have throat problems again – at least, not from singing. Make sure that you don't rely on the throat for vibrato (that will develop naturally and gently, unless you force it); instead, rely on the diaphragm – it will never let you down.

Exercises 10–11

GUIDANCE NOTES

Pronunciation

'Mee-yaa' – Use the tongue to push the jaw right down on 'yaa' and focus the sound in the nose. This is essential.

The object is to achieve as much power from the diaphragm as possible by pulling it in sharply on every note, so it must be *loud*. Most people find these exercises very difficult, and you may need to practise them for a long time, but even if you don't get it right, making a serious attempt at it will give your voice tremendous support throughout your range, taking pressure away from the throat. Most singers who have mastered these exercises say they never suffer from sore throats now. I presume that they mean not from singing, anyway!

For the fast versions, move the diaphragm violently in order to motivate the notes. One movement on every single note: that's the objective. Make sure that it really is your diaphragm that you're moving (from inside) and not just your chest and shoulders that are bouncing up and down. At first, you may need to use your hands to manipulate your diaphragm at the speed required. Place your hands on your stomach (clenching your fists can be helpful here) and really use them to shake your front abdominal muscles. Don't just bat the outside.

For the slow version, slam the diaphragm in hard at the start of every note (gentleness will get you nowhere in these two exercises) and then relax it. Do the same for every note, trying to work up a rhythm. Make sure that you make a loud sound when you pull the diaphragm in – let the voice thunder. You may need to *act* the connection between the voice and the diaphragm at first; don't expect it to work like magic.

Keep your head down throughout, or the throat will start to take the pressure off the diaphragm, which is like the tail wagging the dog.

Also, don't let the jaw creep up on 'yaa'; push it down with the tip of the tongue, or the throat will take over, you will lose the focus and the sound will be woolly.

There must be no Hs or silences, as these allow the throat to play too active a part. Instead, all of the articulation must be achieved by the diaphragm.

Don't fall into the trap of controlling the articulation by clicking in the throat as if you were singing Handel's *Messiah*. You're not supposed to be practising delicate coloratura (which *can* be done by clicking in the throat, although I wouldn't advise it); instead, you're preparing for spectacular rock singing by exercising the voice with the power muscles.

Exercise 10: Power And Speed From The Diaphragm

Do this three times: First time fast
Second time slow
Third time fast

Exercise 11: Vibrato From The Power Muscles

Read the Guidance Notes on pages 67–9.

This is not the only way of achieving vibrato, but it is the most reliable. This exercise need not be done very fast; go fast enough to give it a strong rhythmic drive. However, it must be *loud.*

26
ee - ee - ee - ee - ee.
Yaa - aa - aa - aa - aa
- aa - aa - aa - aa - aa
- aa - aa - aa - aa - aa -
30
aa-aa-aa-aa-aa
- aa-aa-aa-aa-aa
Yaa-aa-aa-aa-aa
- aa-aa-aa-aa-aa
- aa-aa-aa-aa-aa-
35
aa - aa - aa - aa - aa
- aa - aa - aa - aa - aa.
Mee - ee - ee - ee - ee
- ee - ee - ee - ee - ee -
39
ee-ee-ee-ee-ee
- ee-ee-ee-ee-ee
- ee-ee-ee-ee-ee.
Mee-ee-ee-ee-ee
- ee-ee-ee ee-ee-
44
ee - ee - ee - ee - ee
- ee - ee - ee ee - ee
- ee - ee - ee - ee - ee.
Yaa - aa - aa - aa - aa -

48
aa-aa-aa-aa-aa - aa-aa-aa-aa-aa - aa-aa-aa-aa-aa - aa-aa-aa-aa-aa. Yaa-aa-aa-aa-aa -
53
aa - aa - aa - aa - aa - aa - aa - aa - aa - aa - aa - aa - aa - aa - aa - aa - aa - aa - aa - aa.
57
Mee-ee-ee-ee-ee - ee-ee-ee-ee-ee - ee-ee-ee-ee-ee - ee-ee-ee-ee-ee - ee-ee-ee-ee-ee.
62
Mee - ee - ee - ee - ee - ee - ee - ee - ee - ee - ee - ee - ee - ee - ee - ee - ee - ee - ee - ee -
66
ee - ee - ee - ee - ee. Yaa - aa - aa - aa - aa - aa - aa - aa - aa - aa - aa - aa - aa - aa - aa -

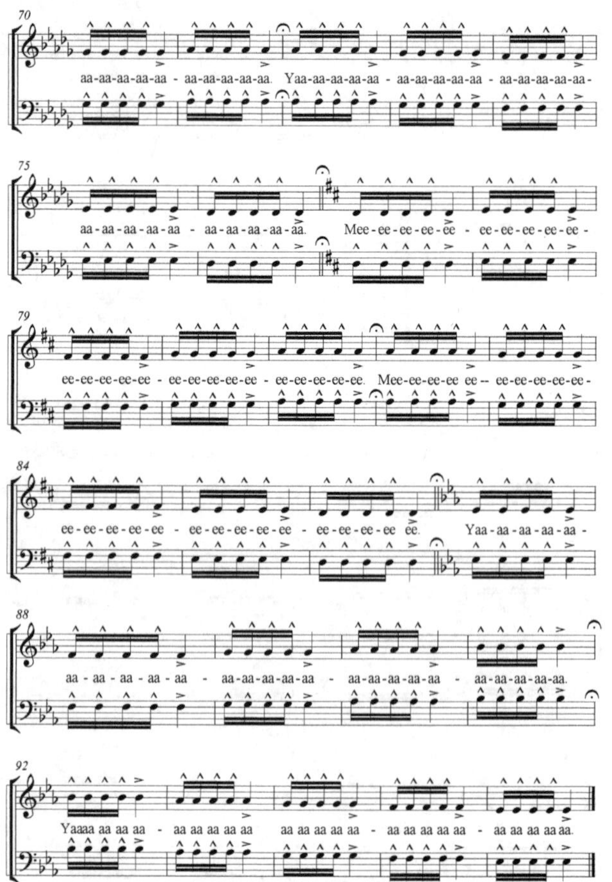
70
aa-aa-aa-aa-aa - aa-aa-aa-aa-aa. Yaa-aa-aa-aa-aa - aa-aa-aa-aa-aa - aa-aa-aa-aa-aa-
75
aa - aa - aa - aa - aa - aa - aa - aa - aa - aa. Mee - ee - ee - ee - ee - ee - ee - ee - ee - ee -
79
ee-ee-ee-ee-ee - ee-ee-ee-ee-ee - ee-ee-ee-ee-ee. Mee-ee-ee-ee ee -- ee-ee-ee-ee-ee-
84
ee - ee - ee - ee - ee - ee - ee - ee - ee - ee - ee - ee - ee - ee ee. Yaa - aa - aa - aa - aa -
88
aa - aa - aa - aa - aa - aa-aa-aa-aa-aa - aa-aa-aa-aa-aa - aa-aa-aa-aa-aa.
92
Yaaaa aa aa aa - aa aa aa aa aa aa aa aa aa aa - aa aa aa aa aa - aa aa aa aa aa.

Exercise 12: Even More Power From The Diaphragm

GUIDANCE NOTES

This is a longer and more demanding version of Exercise 10, so it might be a good idea to re-read the Guidance Notes for Exercise 10 on pages 51–2. One big difference between this one and the previous diaphragm exercises is that most of this one can't really be done slowly; you need to take a run at it, as you will discover.

This exercise is loud – fortissimo. If you try to sing it quietly, it will fall apart. As with all loud singing, you must keep your head down, or it will all go onto the throat: disaster!

The top note of each group or phrase must be the loudest note, and very obviously so. Pull the diaphragm in extra hard on this note. You'll find that the top note will hold this very difficult exercise together.

Pay particular attention to the accents. ^ means 'pull the diaphragm in'; when a note has two accents, ^ and >, give the diaphragm an extra kick to get the mechanism started. (You'll notice that the lowest notes in each phrase aren't accented at all. This is to allow you to relax on the first note of each rising scale, ready to give the second note an extra wallop.)

On these fast-articulated scales, it's easier to control everything when you're going up than when you're coming down. This is because rising pitches require increasing tension, which helps you to hold it all together, but the falling pitches require you to slacken the tension, which can allow it all to fall apart. Your brain sorts out the tension for you subconsciously – you don't have to do anything apart from operate the diaphragm while singing the notes. That's quite enough to occupy anyone's consciousness.

One big advantage of the lack of tension in the lower scales is that you can slow them down (from bar 40 onward). Here, co-ordination becomes easier. You can go slow enough to move the diaphragm on every single note. At this pitch (having stretched the soft palate and worked up the tension on the highest scales – you must do the high ones first), you can now work up the technique in slow motion and make it perfect, ready to do the higher scales again. The rubric in the notation is quite clear about this.

Don't worry if you can't get this exercise together quickly. Just keep trying.

Exercise 12

This is very difficult and will test your technique to the limit. Read the Guidance Notes for this exercise.

Push the jaw down on 'yaa' or the throat will start helping out the diaphragm, which is the tail wagging the dog.

Few ladies will be able to continue in the chest voice further than this.
Do so if you can, otherwise cut to bar 40.

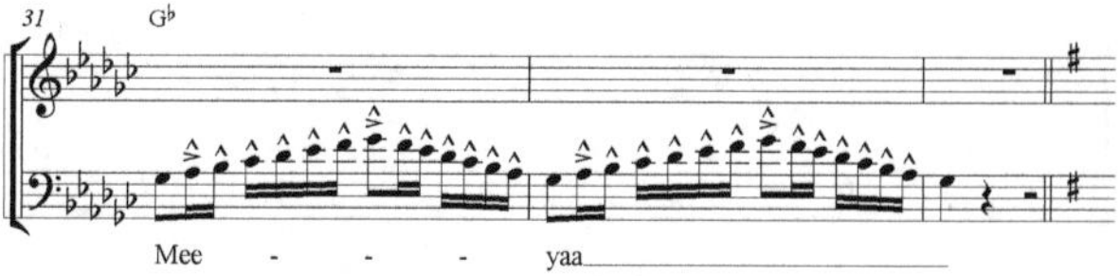

31
G♭
Mee - - - yaa

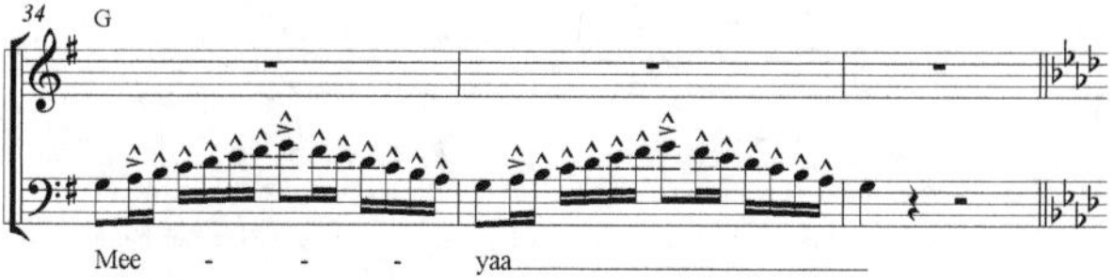

34
G
Mee - - - yaa

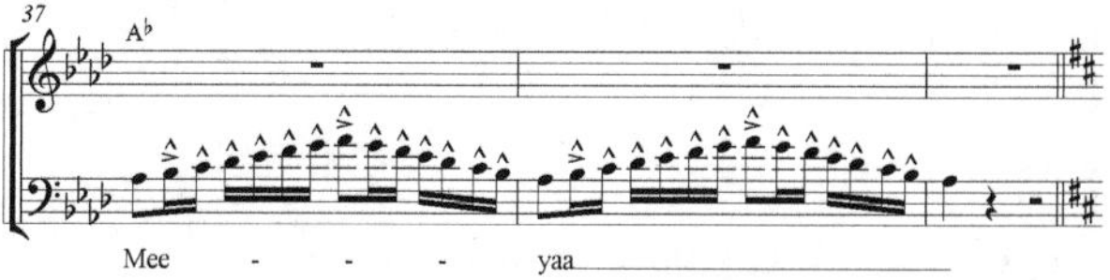

37
A♭
Mee - - - yaa

Now go back down, reversing the order of the phrases. The ladies rejoin here:

40
D
Mee - - - yaa

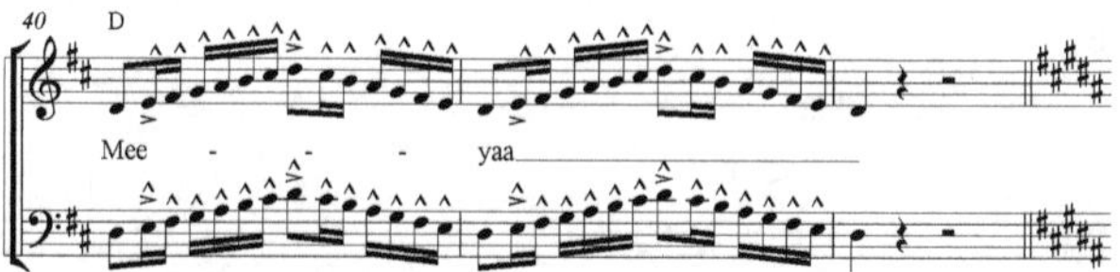

Continue downward through the scales until you get to here. Now slow it right down. At this pitch, you can really move the diaphragm on every single note.

Much slower. Look at the change in the notation.
43
B
Mee - - - - - - - yaa

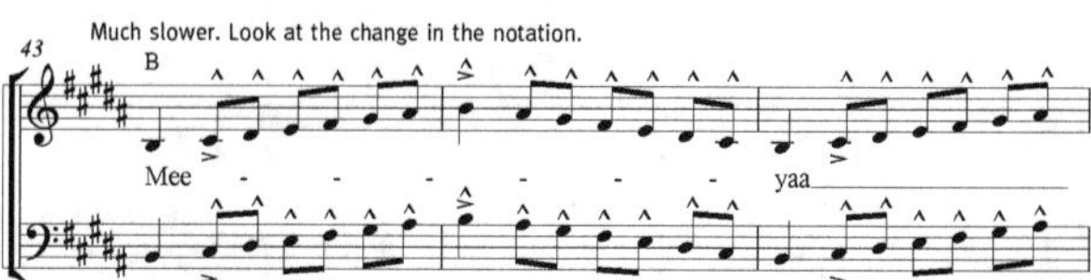

46
B♭
Mee
49
yaa
Relax on the lowest note. Do an extra-hard pull on the diaphragm on the second note of each rising scale marked ›.
52
A
Mee
55
yaa
58
A♭
Mee
yaa
61
G
Mee

64

yaa

68 G♭

Mee - - - - yaa

72 F

Mee - - - - yaa

76 E

Mee - - -

80 E♭

yaa

Mee -

84

- - yaa

basic Vocal Workout

Now start to come up.

F

A little faster.

Faster. Watch your technique with the diaphragm.

Back up to speed.

5 BRINGING THE CHEST VOICE UP TO THE HIGH NOTES

This is part of the process of joining up the voices, and very hard work it is, too, but all my students seem to enjoy it. You can really feel the power. (That sounds like a quote from *MTV*!) Broadly speaking, women have two voices, head voice and chest voice, while men have three: natural head voice, falsetto head voice and chest voice.

Bringing the chest voice up to meet and blend with the head voice gives warmth and richness to the entire voice, as well as a general increase in power. It means that, however quietly and gently you sing, however 'throwaway' your style, your voice will never sound trivial.

You should make sure that the chest voice is well exercised before you try this. Always do some of the earlier chest voice and diaphragm exercises first so that you start with a good deep chest sound and, therefore, have something to take up to the high notes. Exercise 12 is also good for this, which is why I have put the two exercises close together.

Men may find that Exercises 11 and 12 will work better after they've learned to do some of the quiet mixed head voice exercises. Everyone should certainly work the chest voice alongside the head voice, but don't try to alternate them. When men are going to be working on both voices on the same day, it's important that they do the chest-voice exercises first, before they move on to the mixed head voice. Women, on the other hand, should perform the head-voice exercises first.

Contrary to popular belief, singers should usually do the big, heavy exercises before they move on to the lighter, more delicate stuff. This is where the big mistakes are made in warm-ups: too many teachers start with gentle exercises, so no real stretching is done. With Exercises 12 and 13, start with 'may, may, may' (Exercise 1). The women should then do the highest 'koos' (the downward scales) that they can manage and then go on to the chest-voice exercises. The men, meanwhile, should go from 'may, may, may' straight to the chest-voice exercises. Everybody is then ready for Exercises 12 and/or 13. After all that, the delicate exercises (most of which are for *blending* your different voices) can be used to smoothe down the whole voice so that you can build on the tone quality you've gained from all that stretching and thundering.

Exercise 13: Vocal Thunder From The Diaphragm

All the notes in this exercise are important. Do not regard any of them as being of less importance than any of the others. And they should all be *loud*.

GUIDANCE NOTES

This is a great voice builder. Keep your head fairly well down throughout – this is a loud and demanding exercise, so you don't want any pressure to go onto the throat. Keep your tongue against your bottom teeth throughout as an added precaution, *even when you're taking a breath.*

Pronunciation

- **Mee** – keep the lips fairly closed. You might find it helpful to pull the corners of the lips back slightly, which will focus the sound in the nose and (hopefully) stop you using the throat.

- **Yaa** – this should be as open as possible. Push the jaw down with the tongue, again focusing the sound in the nose. This applies to *all* of the 'yaas', not just the one on the top note. Remember, *every* note is important in this exercise. Make good use of the Y of 'yaa'. Wallow in it. This will help you to position everything correctly. This exercise is difficult enough when you're using all of your technique; don't make it more difficult by forgetfulness or laziness.

Pull in the diaphragm hard on both of the top notes (marked ^), then slide down to the next note (marked with a *trill* – a squiggly line over the note). Don't drop suddenly, or the voice will change in the throat. Then release the diaphragm and shake it, thus making the sound of the trill. (You should be able to work up a nice vibrato from the diaphragm in this exercise.) Then take a breath, ready for the last part.

Start the last part of the phrase at the same volume at which you finished the trill – don't start it quieter. Pull in the diaphragm on the first note (marked ^), which has now become the highest note in that phrase, and finish the exercise with a good resonant sound.

As this exercise goes higher and higher, you'll need all the support you can get. Push the jaw right down on the most difficult notes – this takes a lot of courage. Make full use of the diaphragm. You'll need to constipate the highest notes: this exercise is so demanding that you need to use *everything*.

Keep it all entirely in the chest voice. Don't let it go into the head voice at all.

Exercise 13

This is a demanding exercise. Read the Guidance Notes.

^ means *pull the diaphragm in hard.*
w means *shake the diapragm* to produce some vibrato.
sfz means *sforzando.*

Bringing The Chest Voice Up To The High Notes

basic Vocal Workout

Few ladies will be able to sing as high as this without going into the head voice.
Those of you who can, continue an octave higher than the men.

Keep your head down here, or it will go onto the throat:

Constipate like mad for the top notes:

6 MAGICAL SOUNDS IN THE MALE MIXED HEAD VOICE

This is a peculiarity of the male voice. Although a similar technique is often beneficial in female voices (I shall come to that in the next section), it doesn't produce the same effect. This is because the quiet mixed head voice is the perfect mixture of the falsetto head voice and the natural head voice. The difference between these two voices (and, therefore, the possibility of blending them) doesn't occur in the female voice.

It is made almost entirely in the sinuses. Singers often go dizzy or light-headed when they do this, partly because they are intoxicated with the sounds – magical!

There are two ways of getting at your top notes: loudly and quietly. What a surprise! You need both. Until now, we've looked at the loud approach; the mixed head voice is the quiet technique. It is one of the great problem-solvers. If your voice refuses to go up to the high notes that you so desperately want, if people (including some singing teachers) tell you that you'll never get up above an F or a G, for instance, because you're a baritone or a bass, then this is the technique you need. Eventually, it *will* produce the goods. It's the most difficult technique of all for the male singer, but don't let that worry you. Persevere. Your entire voice will benefit from the attempt long before you master it, which may take years.

Most of the previous exercises in this book are about range and power; this section is mostly about tone quality, although it will also increase your range. The mixed head voice is the most valuable of all the voices available to you. It can turn a good singer into a great one, because it allows you to choose and control your sounds. Nearly all of the great rock and pop singers have relied on it for their most seductive vocal moments. You don't need to be born with a magical voice; you just need to do a lot of hard work.

However, the unfairness of it is that, while you're working your guts out to master it, there's always another lucky sod who (apparently!) gets it together without doing any work. That's life!

The quiet mixed head voice can be tackled alongside the previous exercises, but ideally you should have achieved some power in both the natural and falsetto voices before trying to join them up in these exercises. Don't try to alternate these exercises with the loud ones;

do the loud exercises first – get them out of the way – and then devote yourself to the mixed head voice.

Exercise 14: Men Mixing Their Head Voices – Quiet Koos

This is similar in shape to Exercise 6, the loud 'koos', but with a very different style and purpose – this one is quiet. Read the guidance notes carefully. This exercise is about 300 years old, and nobody has been able to devise a better one for the purpose. The pitch is appropriate for modern rock; operatic tenors would start slightly lower.

GUIDANCE NOTES

Do Exercise 6 (the loud 'koos') first. Ease your head right back – don't jerk it – and stick out your jaw, stretching the front of your neck and smoothing out any veins or pipes that seem determined to be tense. You don't want the carotid arteries standing out like drainpipes.

When you first do this exercise, it's likely to be a fight between your jaw and your neck, but the jaw must win. You'll gradually learn to do this without any pressure on the neck at all. Watch your neck in the mirror while you do it.

Sing the first scale quietly entirely in falsetto. Keep your tongue against your bottom teeth. The first note must be absolutely in tune – a tiny squeak, not merely an escape of air. You may need to help the first note of some scales by squeezing the diaphragm, or by constipating slightly.

In the subsequent scales, change on the note indicated by the asterisk (*) into the mixed voice. At first, the mixed voice is merely a quiet version of the natural voice, but as you persevere it will take on the smooth focus of your own distinctive mixed voice. This may take a long time. You'll know when you're getting it right: you'll hear it 'ring', and you'll be very dizzy. It is called the head voice for good reasons!

Don't try to change voices on the second note of any scale – it's almost impossible to keep it in tune.

You might need to go slightly louder on the 'change note' (the first note in the mixed voice in each scale). Here is a paradox: if you sing the change note too loudly, you'll blow yourself off the note; if you're not loud enough, you won't get hold of the note at all, which will force you into a second, unwanted change further down the scale. You want only one change of voice in any scale. Eventually, you'll develop a specific awareness of the right volume for every single note. (This is different for everybody.)

Repeat the whole exercise endlessly. Magic takes time.

Magical Sounds In The Male Mixed Head Voice

Exercise 14

Exercises 15–18: Looking After The Easy Part Of The Male Voice

This aspect of singing is often neglected. We're so keen to tackle the spectacular sounds that we forget about those light, pleasant, throwaway sounds, so that none of our singing ever really sounds easy; it always sounds like heavy weather. This is how to tackle it. It's particularly useful if you're finding the other mixed-voice exercises very difficult.

Don't scorn the boy-band sounds; they won't stop you from producing the dirtier sounds of hard rock, death or metal. Far from it, indeed – they'll make the transition from one type of sound to another a lot easier, provided that you do the harder sounds first. But feel free to scorn the singers who *only* sing boy-band sounds!

All the notes in this exercise are easy. They're supposed to be. Sing it a dozen times or so in quick succession, then go back to the other mixed-voice exercises. They should then be a little more accessible.

IMPORTANT: This mustn't replace the other mixed-voice exercises, particularly not Exercise 14.

GUIDANCE NOTES

Do at least one loud exercise first (Exercise 1, 'may, may

may', for preference), then do Exercise 14 at least twice before you relax into this one.

Keep your head back so that the sinuses come fully into play. They are essential for producing magical sounds.

Sing very gently, but focus the sound. Go for *nice* sounds. Make them sound easy – boy-band stuff.

Change into the mixed voice wherever it feels most comfortable. This is the only difficult thing in this exercise. Don't leave the change too late, or you'll find that a nasty jolt is forced on you, but don't make the change too early, either, or it will sound difficult.

Remember that, in any phrase or scale, even when it's all supposed to be quiet, the top note should still be the loudest, so don't fall into the trap of starting so quietly that there's nowhere left to go and then being forced to go far too loud after the change. That will tell everyone that you've changed voices. No one's supposed to know. It should be so smooth that it all sounds like one continuous, easy voice – and, eventually, it will be.

Sing this exercise over and over again. If it seems to be getting worse, give it a rest and come back to it; you'll find it a lot smoother.

Exercise 15: Making The Male Voice Sound Beautifully Easy

Start in falsetto and finish quietly in the natural or mixed voice.

Sostenuto (very gently and smoothly). Change where it feels most comfortable.

It's all very easy, except for the change note.

Try to make the change so smooth that it sounds like one continuous voice.

Keep your head back throughout, and keep your tongue against your bottom teeth.

If it hurts, you're doing too much. Keep it gentle but focused. Watch the tuning.

Do the last two scales entirely in the mixed voice, quietly.

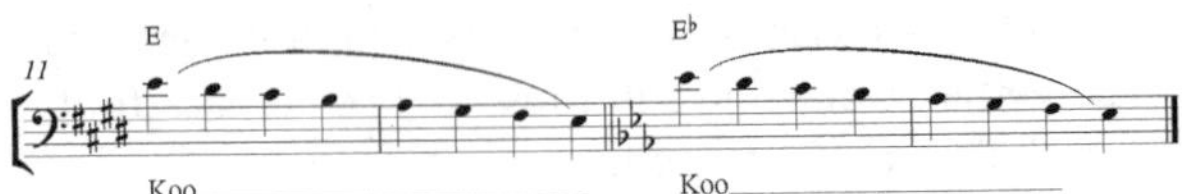

Exercise 16: Male Mixed Voice Chromatic Half-Scales (Descending)

The same Guidance Notes as for Exercise 14, except for the falsetto, which doesn't occur here at all. Keep your head back and your tongue against your bottom teeth. Do these quietly, entirely in the mixed voice, with no falsetto at all.

You need to take a big breath for these. Squeeze the diaphragm towards the end of each rising scale. Keep it all in the mixed voice

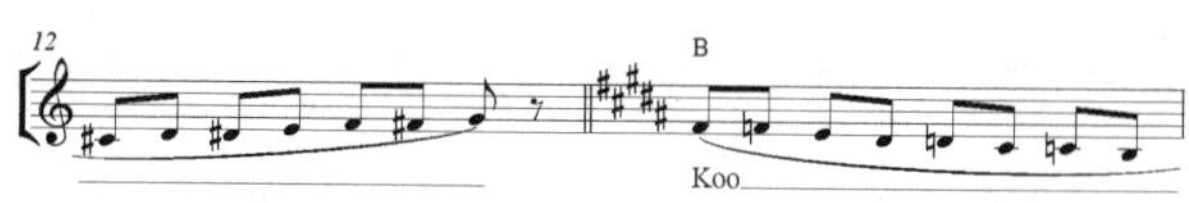

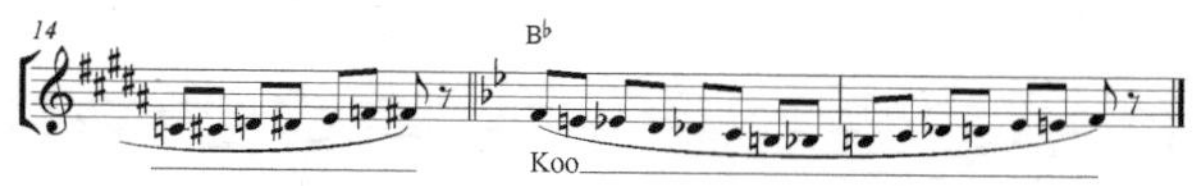

Exercise 17: Chromatic 12-Tone Scales In The Male Mixed Voice

Ease your head back and keep your tongue against your bottom teeth.

Exercise 18: Darkening The Sound Of The Male Mixed Voice

The Guidance Notes here are basically the same as for Exercises 14-17, plus:

i Do this entirely in the mixed voice. Don't allow it to go into falsetto at all.
ii As you go higher, you'll need to start each scale slightly louder than the previous one.
iii Remember to keep your head back and your tongue against your bottom teeth, or you'll go into the chest voice, which will defeat the object of the exercise.

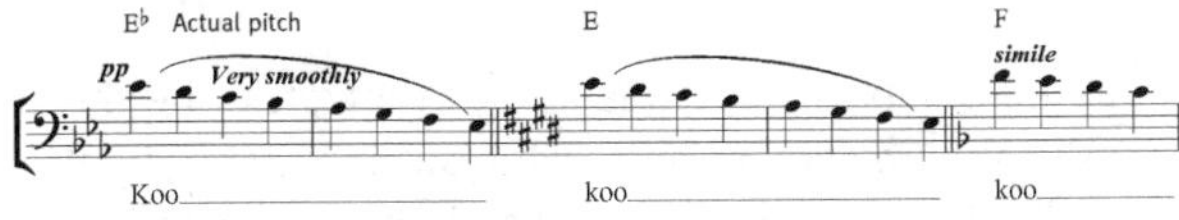

From here on you may need to go quite a lot louder on the first note — ONLY the first!

It's perfectly possible to bring the male mixed voice up to here. It usually takes about four years...and some excruciatingly hard work!

7 THE FEMALE MIXED VOICE

Quiet, Smooth Sounds

The quiet mixed voice was always thought to be the exclusive province of men, who can mix the natural head voice with the falsetto head voice. In women's voices there is really only one head voice, so in theory there should be nothing to mix. Recently, however, women have begun to produce an unmistakably mixed voice in the so-called *feigned voice*, the overlap of the head and chest voices. It is a wonderful sound and entirely new, characterised by a smooth, velvety focus. Unlike the male mixed head voice, which is by far the most difficult technique in singing, the female mixed voice is easy: you just need persistence. It's formed almost entirely in the sinuses, which means that any form of struggling for notes in the following exercises defeats it. This doesn't mean that you shouldn't continue to struggle for notes in the bigger, more demanding, exercises. You *must* do the power exercises first, stretching the range of both head voice and chest voice, or you'll have nothing very much to mix in the mixed voice.

I discovered this voice almost by accident. One of my students asked me if there was a way to soften those very loud notes at the top of the chest voice without switching into the head voice. It was obviously worth exploring, as the gentleness required precluded any risk of forcing the voice, and in any case she had developed the full range and was expert at power singing. So I devised the following exercises, some of which are adapted from fairly ancient exercises for quiet singing in the male voice. Within a few weeks, she was able to soften the high chest-voice notes without losing the focus or the tone – in fact, the tone was improving. Within a few months, it had developed into an unmistakably mixed voice. So I tried it with several other students with similar gratifying results.

Most of the previous exercises in this book are about range and power, whereas this part is mostly about tone quality. You may not notice any difference for a few weeks or even months; as with every singing technique, some people learn it more quickly than others. The quiet mixed voice can be tackled alongside the previous exercises but, ideally, you should have achieved some power in both the head voice and the chest voice before you try to blend them in these exercises. Don't try to alternate these exercises with the loud ones; make sure you do the loud exercises first – get them out of the way – and then devote yourself to the mixed voice.

This section can also be seen as looking after the easy sounds of the voice, which are often neglected. We're often so busy tackling the virtuoso sounds and techniques in our ambition to sing higher, lower, louder, etc, that we forget those crucial, gentle sounds, so that our singing always sounds like a tremendous effort. These exercises will help you when you want your singing to sound effortless.

Exercises 19–24: The Female Mixed Voice

First, be aware that, although some of these exercises look like Exercise 5 in reverse, they employ very different techniques.

GUIDANCE NOTES

First, do all the usual warm-up exercises, especially Exercise 5. Make sure that the range is fully exercised, both head voice and chest voice, or you won't have anything to mix. Ease your head right back – don't jerk it – and stick out your jaw, stretching the front of your neck and smoothing out any veins or pipes that seem determined to be tense. All of the notes must be easy; if they aren't, you're doing too much of something and probably singing too loud.

Stick your lips out a little bit, causing a tunnel forward and back in your mouth and throat. You can't push your jaw down in this exercise. Keep your tongue against your bottom teeth or bottom gum throughout. Think 'Chest voice!', but don't force it into the chest voice: just *think* it. Let the voice change where it wants to, but try to smoothe over the changes.

Make sure that you're absolutely in tune. The intonation here is crucial. You might need to help the first note of each scale by squeezing the diaphragm, or by constipating slightly – just on the first note. You may also need to squeeze the diaphragm again on the last two or three notes of some scales, just to stop them from fading out. Quiet singing must still be audible, so maintain the focus – quietly. It must all be easy.

There must be no jolts between the notes, particularly between the first and second notes, which is where the worst jolt usually occurs). Slide from note to note, but keep it all in tune. If the tuning is at all difficult, even when you follow these instructions, either you're trying to sing too loudly or you need to take bigger breaths.

Repeat the whole exercise endlessly. You may not notice any difference for several weeks, or even several months.

Exercise 19: Softening The High Notes Of The Female Chest Voice

Read the Guidance Notes for this section. Sometimes you'll need to do the whole of this exercise, starting from bar 1 and going on to bar 20. At other times you'll want to concentrate on the distinctive tone of one particular part, but at first I recommend that you begin at Part 2.

Part 1

If you need to darken the voice, start here and continue up to bar 18.
Keep your head back, sing very gently and focus your voice by putting the tip of the tongue against your bottom gum.

Part 2

Start here. This is the section you need to do most.
Keep your head right back, and do this very quietly.

Let the voice change where it wants to change, but try to smoothe over the jolts.

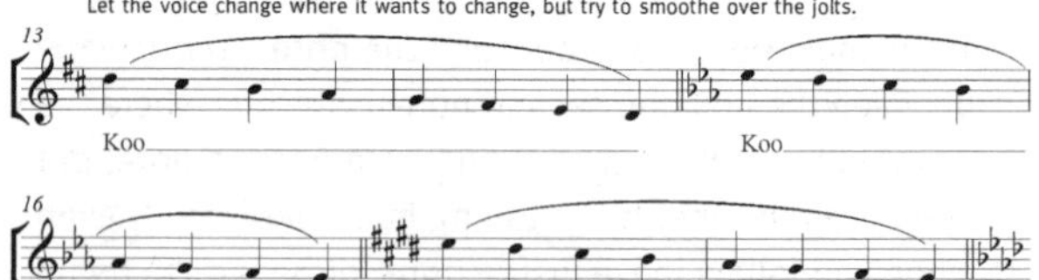

Part 3

This section should be used very sparingly, but it's useful if the voice feels a bit stiff or difficult in Parts 1 or 2. Continue up from bar 18, semitione by semitone, until you get to here. Keep it all very easy.

Exercise 20: Crossing Between Female Head Voice And Chest Voice

Read the Guidance Notes for this section.

Note: *port* is short for *portamento*, which, musically, means slide.

There must be no gaps, jolts or silences between the notes here. Keep it very smooth and quiet. Don't worry about what voice you're in or try to keep it all in one voice. Let it change where it wants to. Just keep it all very easy.

Exercise 21: Chromatic Half-Scales In The Female Mixed Voice

Exercise 22: Chromatic Half-Scales In The Female Mixed Voice (Descending)

Read the Guidance Notes for this section.

Squeeze the diaphragm for the last few notes. You may need to bend over slightly to squeeze out the last drop of air. You may also need to increase the volume slightly for the last few notes.

Exercise 23: Chromatic 12-Tone Scales In The Female Mixed Voice

Read the Guidance Notes for this section.

8 JOINING UP THE LOUD VOICES

When you've worked extensively on both halves of the voice, doing lots of exercises that focus on the different aspects of the head voice, and you've explored the large variety of purposes of the chest voice, you might feel that you'd like to do some exercises involving the whole voice all at once.

This is advanced stuff. You need to make sure that both halves are working really well. We've already done some work on this with Exercises 12–13, and it might be a good idea to do one of those again before you tackle the exercises in this section.

Exercise 24: 'Nee-yaa-vaa-ee'

GUIDANCE NOTES

Take a big breath, big enough to support the last three notes of this huge phrase. The diaphragm won't support you without such a full breath.

Keep the tongue firmly against the bottom teeth from the introductory breath before you sing onwards.

There must be absolutely no movement at all in the throat or on the outside of the neck – no pipes, no outside plumbing, and no appearance of the carotid arteries. If any of this happens, you haven't taken a big enough breath with the diaphragm. (I make no apology for banging on about taking big breaths with the diaphragm here, as this is where you're going to pay for any shortfall in diaphragm control or breathing technique.)

Push the jaw right down on 'yaa' and 'vaa'. Close the jaw on the 'ee' sounds on the first and last notes. The way in which you handle the difference between the very open and very closed sounds will determine whether you get through the exercise without hurting yourself.

The voice will change during 'yaa'. Don't be tempted to close the jaw or the throat at this point – and it is a very strong temptation. Keep your jaw open and take all the strain with the diaphragm as you ease the huge voice through the change. This is the crucial part of this exercise.

Start loudly enough to give you a good start. Crescendo to a massive climax on the top note (be triumphant about it – go for a big, beautiful sound!) and fall back with an erotic, slightly slower, still loud, sustained ending.

Exercise 24

B
C
WOMEN
f
ff
Nee - yaa - vaa - ee.
Nee - yaa - vaa - ee.
MEN
f
ff
5
D♭
D
Nee - yaa - vaa - ee.
Nee - yaa - vaa - ee.
9
E♭
E
Nee - yaa - vaa - ee.
Nee - yaa - vaa - ee.
13
F
Nee - - yaa - - vaa - - ee.

Exercise 25: 'Signorana bella'

This isn't nearly as demanding as Exercise 24. It's very old and has a great many variations: 'Senóra bella', 'Sengorina bella', etc. This version is the most fun and is quite a good substitute for Exercise 1

9 G
Sig - no - ra - na bel - - - - - - - la!
11 A♭
Sig - no - ra - na bel - - - - - - - la!
13 A
Sig - no - ra - na bel - - - - - - - la!
15 B♭
Sig - no - ra - na bel - - - - - - - la!
17 B
Sig - no - ra - na bel - - - - - - - la!

BIBLIOGRAPHY

BEHNKE, Emil: *The Mechanism Of The Human Voice*
(London, J Curwin & Sons, 1880)

The Hutchinson Concise Dictionary Of Music
(Oxford, Helicon Publishing Ltd, 1998)

MARCHESI, Mathilde: *Marchesi's Vocal Method*
(London, Edwin Ashdown Ltd)

MILLER, Richard: *The Structure Of Singing, System And Art In Vocal Technique*
(New York, Schirmer Books, 1986)

REID, Cornelius L: *Bel Canto – Principles And Practices*
(New York, Joseph Patelson, 1950)

The Free Voice – A Guide to Natural Singing
(New York, Joseph Patelson, 1965)

Voice – Psyche And Soma
(New York, Joseph Patelson, 1975)